HAPPY

JACK   01-01-'05

mad for road

AIR TIME

Colm Murphy slingshots his Group N Subaru
on the famous Ardgroom stage during the 2004
Killarney Rally of the Lakes.

McGARRITY MOUNTAINEERING
Tarmac Champion Derek McGarrity
climbs Knockalla during the 2004
Donegal International Rally.

mad for road

Esler Crawford and Alan Tyndall

THE
BLACKSTAFF
PRESS
BELFAST

ATLANTIC CROSSING

Ron Neilly and Roy Kernaghan on the Atlantic Drive
stage during the 1974 Donegal International Rally

Contents

FLYING FOCUS

Austin McHale and Brian Murphy in their
Ford Focus WRC 03 during the 2004
Killarney Rally of the Lakes

Introduction

The hillsides are alive with expectancy. There are no luxuries out here. Along with other rallying disciples, you have risen at an ungodly hour to travel many miles in often atrocious conditions. Your car's in a ditch, your trainers are letting in, and all to gain a vantage point on a desolate mountainside. Even the local four-legged inhabitants, who are supplied with thick woolly fleeces, have taken cover.

Suddenly the knowledgeable go silent and the wisecrackers take a breath. In the breeze somebody has heard the low drones of a flat-four engine and the gunfire of an anti-lag system. The greatest free show in the country is on its way. With a couple of warning blasts from the marshal's whistle a multi-coloured projectile vaults into sight, dancing across the black stuff on a knife-edge between adhesion and disaster. Its tail trims the ditches, its wheels spray the faithful with mud or dust, depending on the weather. In seconds it's gone, leaving in its wake a crescendo of excited discussion – 'He was lit.' 'She was on the full of the rack.' 'He's the mon to send her on.' 'The knowledge' with his Casio in his hand nods knowingly at his timepiece and pronounces 'plus two'. A second expert appears, according to whom Andrew has made up two seconds on Austin with only a third of the stage completed.

Welcome to Irish tarmac rallying, one of the most enthusiastically followed series in the world. This is a place where there is a special arrangement between the 'haves' and the 'have-nots'. The 'haves' own the cars that the 'have-nots' marvel over. Surprisingly, there are few begrudgers – maybe it's because the 'haves' are so accessible. You can mix with them; touch them; hell, even talk to them! They are men of the people who mingle with the people and they bring their fabulous free speed circus right to the 'have-nots' doors. Their racetracks are our backyards and their cars at least bear some resemblance to our everyday wheels. They deal with road hazards that we can understand, and we love to watch them because they dare to do what most of us can only dream of.

Sure, there is resentment that many talented drivers never have the opportunity to develop their skills because of the financial frustrations that shadow this sport. There are scores of clubmen who have the speed but not the bank balance, and scores more who have had the bank balance but not the speed. Of those who have become rally stars, not all come from the upper income bracket. Many have made enormous personal sacrifices to participate, and they certainly never become wealthy from their rallying activities in Ireland.

Mad for Road is not intended as a definitive history of Irish stage rallying. It is a look through Esler Crawford's magical lens at the drivers who have mastered the tarmac in Ireland, north and south, since the 1950s. It tells the stories and captures the passion that drives the fans and the thousands of volunteers who often endure extreme conditions to witness 'their man' in action.

8   **Billy Coleman and Ronan Morgan's Porsche 911 SCRS
on the Circuit of Ireland in 1986**

Tackling the terminology

Rallying today is really quite simple. The fastest *crew* (driver and co-driver) over the *special stages* (sections of roads closed to the public) is the winner. The crews are allowed to *recce* (drive at slow speeds through these stages) and make *pace notes* (instructions to warn the driver of the hazards) during limited and specified periods before the rally. During the rally their mechanics are allowed to repair the cars in *service areas* (car parks designated by the organisers), but only in these designated areas. Competitors must obey all road traffic requirements between special stages.

FTD (fastest time of the day) refers to the fastest recorded time on a stage. A *bogie time* is when a competitor exceeds the maximum average speed allowed on a stage by the *FIA* (see below). *OTL* (out of time limit) is when a crew exceeds its time allowance (usually fifteen minutes at most) into or out of a control point. *Road penalties* accrue when a crew clocks into a control point too early or too late. *Road books* are provided by the organisers; they tell the crews what routes to take between stages and what times they are allowed. *Time controls* must be visited along the route, and at the exact time specified in the road book.

FIA (Fédération Internationale de l'Automobile), *MSA* (Royal Automobile Motor Sports Association Limited) and *MSI* (Motorsport Ireland) are the people who look after the sport internationally, in the UK and in the Republic of Ireland respectively. *TROA* (Tarmac Rally Organisers Association), established by representatives of all the qualifying rounds of the Irish Tarmac Rally Championship, promotes this series.

WRC stands for World Rally Championship or World Rally Car. *Group N* are the slightly modified production models. A *Special* usually means a car that has been modified by the owner or another engineer to adapt it to specific tasks. *Modified*, as the name suggests, means the more radically tuned cars. *2WD* means two-wheel-drive; *4WD*, four-wheel-drive; *FWD*, front-wheel-drive; *RWD*, rear-wheel-drive. *Homologation* is the approval for a car to compete in a certain class. A *works driver* is employed by the manufacturers to drive their competition car. A *works car* is supplied by the manufacturer for competition purposes.

Now you're an expert!

Trials and tribulations

The 1903 Automobile Fortnight, organised by the Automobile Club of Great Britain and Ireland, was a colossal affair. It included the Gordon Bennett Races on the Athy circuit in County Kildare; speed trials in Dublin's Phoenix Park and on the Carrigrohane Straight in Cork; and hillclimbs at Castlewellan, County Down, and in Kerry. It is hard to imagine how difficult it would have been, over a hundred years ago, to get to these diverse locations, let alone take part in the events!

Those two weeks gave birth to motorsport in Ireland. As time went by the racers graduated to purpose-built circuits, while the open road remained the challenge for rallymen. Initially endurance and navigation skills were at a premium, but these days speed, and only speed, is the priority.

The 1903 event paved the way for the Irish Reliability Trials, which ran from 1906 to 1909. They were typical of the pioneering events. H.M. Buist captured their spirit in the June 1909 edition of *The Motor World* magazine when he wrote:

> The more agreeable turn of speed allowed on the Irish Trial made it possible to arrive at each night's destination at a reasonable hour. In Ireland you enjoy yourself, no matter how abominable the weather.

By 1909 the Trial had increased from four to six days and, foreshadowing the Circuit of Ireland some twenty-seven years later, it circulated around the country. The cars were classified according to their selling prices and, as today, there were amateur and trade-supported drivers.

The long runs were interspersed with hillclimbs, and on one occasion a speed trial on Magilligan Strand in County Londonderry. Reliability in those days was almost non-existent. In the Royal Automobile Club's records, the stoppages on the Cork to

STRANDED
Captain Lindsay Know in his Orleans leads the Earl of Shrewsbury's Clement-Talbot onto Magilligan Strand for a speed trial during the 1907 Irish Automobile Club's Reliability Trial.

Killarney run during the 1908 event are documented:

> After a mile a German stopped with an engine problem. At two miles a Cadillac and a Chambers were also in engine difficulties, and the Chambers had a dropped lamp bracket. After thirty-two miles a Calthorpe was stopped and needed its gear lever adjusted. Forty-seven miles along the road and a Phoenix had a broken rear spring, and close to Killarney a Berliet needed a chain repaired. A Rover, Royal Starling, Darracq and De Dion had retired and a Minerva and a Daimler had turned over!

Everything stopped during the Great War, of course, but by the 1930s things were beginning to stir in the North, where the Ulster Automobile Club (UAC) used the Monte Carlo Rally format to run the 1931 Ulster Motor Rally. As on the Monte Carlo circuit there were various starting points. Sixty-three cars started from Belfast, three from Bantry, six from Dover, four from John O'Groats and one from Land's End. This was the forerunner to the Circuit of Ireland Trial, which ran under that title for the first time in 1936 and became the sport's leading event in this country. Over the years the Circuit had various starting and finishing points, but Killarney became its base and social centre.

Basil Clarke was the first person to have his name etched on the UAC Challenge Trophy as winner of the Circuit of Ireland in 1936. His crew included one Ronnie Adams, who would go on to achieve considerable international success, including a victory in the blue-ribbon event, the Monte Carlo Rally.

The light-hearted nature of the early rallies is highlighted by a Dr Loughridge's admission in 1934 that his reason for entering the Circuit was to deliver an Easter egg to his niece in Enniskillen!

After the Second World War our noble rally adventurers began to gather again, with their petrol coupons in their hands. This was an era of great engineering ingenuity, as vehicles, like petrol, were in short supply.

The Lisburn sheep farmer Wilbert Todd was one of those 'first principle' home-engineering geniuses. He acquired an ex-army staff car, hacked the

HEADING OUT OF HOLYWOOD

D.M. Turner climbs Holywood Hill, County Down, in his Cadillac during the 1908 Irish Automobile Club's Reliability Trial.

Humber in two and turned it into a Special. When the crankshaft broke during the event he simply removed the sump and welded the crank there and then! Wilbert did not finish that year but he won the event in 1953 driving a Dellow.

Christopher Lindsay holds a special place in Irish rallying history as the only man to win the Circuit of Ireland Rally single-handed. With his navigational notes strapped to his knee he drove his Nufor Special round the thousand-mile route in 1949 to achieve this extraordinary solo feat.

But times were changing. In the 1950s Specials were banned, and what used to be a jolly Easter jaunt with a few tests thrown in was fast turning into a much more serious navigational, autotesting and speed competition.

The crossroad autotests were the core element in this era. They required the spectacular use of the 'handbrake turn' and 'nose throw' as the drivers dexterously steered their cars between the pylons; they also presented a major memory teaser as drivers struggled to recall the order and direction in which they were required to visit the various 'garages' and stop lines. Autotesting is an art that has survived to this day and it has generally been regarded as an excellent training ground in car control.

New names were emerging. Derek Johnston won the Circuit in 1952. He would become well known as the BBC's Motoring Correspondent, and he was also part of the Ronnie Adams and Frank Bigger team that won the Monte Carlo rally in 1956.

Mervyn Glover gave Dellow their second victory in 1954, and Robin McKinney, the 1955 and 1956 winner in a Triumph TR2, would use his competitive knowledge to good effect when he later volunteered to run the event.

Cecil Vard and Kevin Sherry were the big names from the Republic of Ireland. Sports cars had been invincible, but when a handicap system was introduced Kevin, a Monaghan motor dealer, drove his VW Beetle to an outright win in 1959 and became the first saloon car driver to take the top prize.

Pat Moss was among the increasing number of visiting celebrities, but a local boy began to appear regularly in the result sheets who was destined to become one of the biggest rally celebrities of all time – Mr P.B. Hopkirk.

The competition may have become keener, but Irish rallying has always managed to retain its sense of humour:

BELTING THROUGH BALLAGHBEAMA

C.J. Cathie in his 12hp Star on the famous Kerry pass during the 1909 Reliability Trial. This road is still used as a stage in the Killarney Rally of the Lakes.

A Circuit competitor arrives in a deserted village late at night in search of directions.

'Excuse me, Guard, is this Ballyhaunis?' enquires the rally driver.
'It is, to be sure, but, by the way, your taillight is not working!' says the Guard.
'Give it a kick and it will go on,' says the rally driver.
'Do you want me to kick in your windscreen as well?' enquires the Guard.
'Why's that?' enquires the rally driver.
'Because your tax is up, son!' is the Guard's parting shot.

Ronnie Adams
1930s–50s

In 1956 it was quite something to have a private charter plane sweep you, your two co-drivers and your bulky Mark VII Jaguar from Monte Carlo to London to feature in the popular TV show *Sunday Night at the London Palladium*. But such was the significance of Ronnie Adams, Frank Bigger and Derek Johnston's victory in the world's most famous rally.

Victory with Basil Clarke in a 16hp Austin on the first Circuit of Ireland Trial some twenty years earlier started a competition career for Ronnie Adams that would last twenty-seven years. Over that time Ronnie drove for the Rootes, Alvis, Rover, Ford, Mercedes and Jaguar works teams. He especially enjoyed the challenge of the East African Safari Rally, in which he first competed in 1958. 'The Safari was a driver's rally, uncluttered by silly driving tests. It was man and machine against the clock over the toughest roads in the world,' he recalled with approval. The son of a wealthy Ulster industrialist, Ronnie was the first rally driver from this part of the world to hit the big time, but his fiery temper often landed him in trouble. On an Alpine rally, when he was supposed to be sharing the wheel of a Rootes Group car with Grand Prix driver Peter Collins, he felt that the circuit ace was not giving him a fair share of the time behind the wheel, so he walked away in mid-event, and was sacked for his impulsive behaviour.

'It was my understanding that we would share the driving, but Collins insisted that I navigate and he drive. When we got to the Alps it was clear that he was not going to relent, so we had a stand-up row and I quit there and then.'

Adams also raced on many of the classic circuits, including the Tourist Trophy races on the Dundrod circuit in Northern Ireland, the Mille Miglia in Italy and the Daily Express Trophy at Silverstone, but it is for his Monte Carlo win that he will always be remembered.

GRACE, PACE AND SPACE

That was the Jaguar slogan when Frank Bigger, Ronnie Adams and Derek Johnston won the 1956 Monte Carlo Rally in a Mark VII Jaguar.

The fifties

Right
BEETLE BELTER

Even before the handicap system, which was introduced in 1959 to give saloons a greater chance of winning over their sports-car rivals, Kevin Sherry's VW Beetle had been a thorn in the flesh for the soft-top drivers. The Monaghan motorman became the first driver to win the Circuit of Ireland in a saloon.

Above

MOSS MOTORING

International show-jumper Pat Moss was as brave in a rally car as she was on a horse. After a poor start on the 1958 Circuit of Ireland, her performances on the Healy Pass and Corkscrew hillclimbs brought Stirling Moss's sister right back into contention, and she took the Ladies' Prize.

Left

GO GO MOBILE

A Gogomobile was a tiny car to choose to tackle such a big event as the Circuit of Ireland.

Left

POACHER TURNED GAMEKEEPER

Robin McKinney, who won the Circuit of Ireland in 1955 and 1956, in action in the type of test that he decided to drop after he took over as Clerk of the Course between 1963 and 1967.

Paddy Hopkirk

1950s–60s

Known by local cognoscenti as Paddy 'Hubcap', Hopkirk truly became a household name across the UK. He chalked up eight international rally wins including the Monte Carlo, the Acropolis (twice), the Tour de France, the Austrian Alpine and the Coupe des Alpes (Alpine Rally). Add to that five wins on our premier event, the Circuit of Ireland, and forty years on he is still one of the best-known names in motor sport.

JUMP TALK

Ford driver Vic Elford (left) and Paddy Hopkirk would both be sidelined on the same jump at Lough Eske during the 1966 Circuit of Ireland.

STAGE START

Hopkirk and co-driver Terry Harryman start the first all-special-stage Circuit in 1966. They were to end it on their roof at Lough Eske.

CONSECUTIVE BEETLES

Paddy Hopkirk (78), Robin McKinney (79) and Roger McBurney (80) present their VW vanguard for the 1954 Circuit. Two generations of McBurneys drove VWs, as Robert (pictured immediately to the right of 80) and Roy followed in their father's tyre treads, competing in Beetles with excellent results.

FORD FIGHT

Their lightweight 1293cc Mini was not enough to beat the Ford Twin-Cam in 1970. Hopkirk and Harryman had to settle for second.

FILM FUN

Paddy Hopkirk as cameraman making *A Dash of the Irish* for Castrol on the 1971 Circuit of Ireland

THE 'POOLER' AND PADDY

Alec Poole and Paddy Hopkirk, winners of the 1990 Pirelli Classic Marathon

MONTE MEN

From left: The winning BMC team, Monte Carlo, 1964. Henry Lydon (co-driver), Paddy Hopkirk and Stuart Turner (team manager).

The Circuit of Ireland wins put Paddy on the map, but like Ronnie Adams it was his Monte Carlo win that made him a motoring legend. Unlike Ronnie, who disliked autotests, Paddy was a master of the handbrake turn, and his big break came when Triumph lent him a Standard 10 to do the RAC Rally; he put his test skills to good effect to lead before breaking a sump.

Paddy won his first Circuit of Ireland in a Triumph TR3A in 1958 but then switched to the Rootes Group Team in 1959 and won a further two Circuits (1961 and 1962) driving Sunbeam Rapiers.

Triumph also brought him to Le Mans in 1961, and during his competition career the Belfast boy would race in many of the classic endurance events including Sebring, Spa and the Targa Floria in Sicily.

The Monte is the event that will always appear at the top of Paddy's memoirs. He was third in the classic winter rally in a Sunbeam Rapier in 1962, despite suffering from the flu. In the rival British Motor Corporation (BMC) team Stuart Turner had taken over as team manager, and he drafted Hopkirk in to join the Finns Rauno Aaltonen and Timo Makinen.

His first outing with the team was on the 1962 Royal Automobile Club (RAC) Rally, where he drove one of the brutal Austin Healey 3000s to second place, but by then the revolutionary Mini had arrived, and it was a motoring marriage – made maybe not in heaven, but in Abingdon.

The world's biggest rally prize came his way in 1964, when David (Paddy's Mini) beat Goliath (Swedish driver Bo Ljungfeldt's massive Ford Falcon) in the Monte Carlo rally. An Irish Monte winner was back on the London Palladium stage, eight years after Adams, Bigger and Johnston had stood in the limelight.

The local hero returned to the Circuit of Ireland three times in Minis, and won in 1965 and 1967. By 1970, when Paddy made his final Circuit appearance, the Ford Escort had become the dominant car. Hopkirk's 1293cc Mini with a special four-pot head, twin Webers and twelve-inch wheels was a last-ditch attempt to beat Roger Clark's Ford Escort Twin-Cam, but technology had moved on and Paddy had to settle for second. At the age of thirty-seven, he decided to pack away his helmet, and into the motoring archives went the records of Ireland's most successful rally driver.

Girl power

Women drivers have not been numerous in Irish rallying, but they have certainly made an impact. Rosemary Smith's name immediately comes to mind, but we have witnessed outstanding driving from some very talented visitors too. Pat Moss came in the 1950s to win the Ladies' Prize on the Circuit of Ireland. Scottish lass Louise Aiken-Walker drove with Ford, Peugeot and Vauxhall in Ireland and progressed to win the Ladies World Rally Championship. The most memorable of them all was diminutive Frenchwoman Michèle Mouton, who tamed the mighty Audi Quattro S2.

TULIP
Rosemary on her publicity tour after she won the Tulip Rally in 1965.

Smith

Rosemary is head and shoulders above other Irish women when it comes to motor sporting achievement.

The stunningly good-looking blonde from Dublin was also stunningly quick in a car, a talent that was quickly recognised by the Rootes Team in the 1960s. Her association with their products brought her to Le Mans in a Sunbeam Alpine, and to a glorious outright victory on the Tulip Rally in Holland driving a Hillman Imp. She remains the only Irish woman to have achieved an outright win on a Continental international rally.

In Ireland she drove for the Lombard & Ulster Team and Dealer Opel Team Ireland. She won many Ladies' Prizes, but her best Circuit outing had to be in 1968, when she was third overall to Roger Clark and Adrian Boyd. To this day she is in demand across the globe at historical rallying events.

NIGHT SERVICE

The Lombard & Ulster boys dance attention on Rosemary during the 1973 Galway International Rally.

SWEET SIXTEEN

Number 16 on the 1973 Galway International Rally in the Lombard & Ulster Team Mark I Escort

Louise Aiken-Walker

1980s–90s

Louise hails from the village of Duns on the Scottish Borders, a hamlet with a remarkable motor sporting heritage.

In addition to being the birthplace of Ladies World Rally Champion Louise Aiken-Walker, Duns is also the home of twice World Racing Champion Jim Clark and of internationally renowned rally driver and former Mitsubishi Team Manager Andrew Cowan.

Louise first appeared on the Irish stages as the result of winning a Ford 'find a female driver' competition. But it was with Vauxhall that she gained the Ladies World Rally Championship crown in 1990.

SCOTTISH ALLIANCE
Jimmy McRae and Louise Aiken-Walker on the 1989 Ulster International Rally

AIRBORNE IN IRELAND
Louise Aiken-Walker and Ellen Morgan in the Group A Vauxhall Astra on the 1989 Circuit. This is the type of car that Aiken-Walker drove to take the Ladies World Rally Championship crown.

Michèle
Mouton
1980s

MIGHTY MOUSE

The mighty S1 Audi Quattro (the most powerful rally car ever seen in Ireland), driven by the tiny Frenchwoman, leaves the start of the 1985 Ulster International Rally.

The girl from Grasse in the south of France is probably the greatest female rally driver of all time.

We never saw the best of Michèle, however, as she came to Ireland in 1985, on the downturn of her career, for the Circuit of Ireland and the Ulster International Rally. Both visits were short-lived and ended in early retirements, but everyone remembers this petite lady who so nearly won the World Rally Championship outright in 1982.

SHORT RUN FOR SHORT QUATTRO
Michèle's 1985 visit to the Circuit of Ireland did not last the first day.

Her successes are legendary –

French Ladies Rally Champion
Five-times European Ladies Rally Champion
Spanish Rally Champion
Outright winner of the Tour de France, San Remo, Portugal and Brazil rallies

23

The. sixties

While the rest of the world went flower-power, the rally world went Mini-mad. The ingenious little Alec Issigonis—designed box was to rallying what the Beatles were to music. As in the world of pop music and fashion, the old order was facing a major revolution.

Driving tests and map reading gradually gave way in the 1960s to special stages and road books, and speed became the priority. New names and new events were emerging, and, led by the Ulster Automobile Club, rallying in Ireland moved into the modern era and to a format that has remained largely unchanged to this day.

There had been numerous navigational events throughout Ireland, the Cork 20 Hours and Circuit of Munster being two of the most renowned, but now the clubs were mixing navigation with special stages and heading towards the all-out speed events that would eventually form the Tarmac International Championship.

MINI BEGINNINGS
Although Roger Clark would become much more synonymous with rear-wheel-drive machines, he made his first appearances in Ireland in Minis. He is seen here climbing the Tim Healy Pass on the 1963 Circuit.

The sport was full of personalities. Paddy O'Callaghan from Kanturk amply filled his VW with his large frame and pipe smoke. Mustachioed Charles Eyre-Maunsell seemed a relic of the 'fighter pilot' age, with his public-school accent and daredevil driving, which usually ended in destruction of one form or another. But it was the personalities from outside the island that were beginning to make their mark in the results, particularly one Roger Albert Clark, though it would be the 1970s before he really came into his own.

SKODAS AND JOE SOAP

Wilbert Todd and Thompson Glass were lent the day-glo Czech cars, and mechanics Jan and Joe Soap, for the 1962 Circuit.

BEETLE DRIVE

As the emphasis switched to speed, the days of the VW were numbered. Ronnie McCartney is seen here on the Tim Healy Pass during the 1961 Circuit of Ireland.

The seventies

The move to special stages was completed in the 1970s, and Galway (1971), Donegal (1972), Ulster (1976), Cork (1977) and eventually Killarney (1979) joined the Circuit of Ireland as full-blown international rallies.

THE TULLYHOMMON FLYER
Mervyn Johnston gets his Mini Cooper S out of shape on the 1973 Circuit.

Donegal driver Robert Ward was preparing his Triumph Dolomite Sprint outside his Kerrykeel garage for the five-day Circuit of Ireland Rally when a local happened by.

'What are you up to, Robert?'

'Oh, I'm off on the Circuit of Ireland next weekend,' replies Robert.

'And where does that go?'

'Well, it starts in Bangor next Friday evening, goes right across the north and down the west coast overnight to Killarney. On Easter Sunday we a loop of the Ring of Kerry. Then on Monday we set off again through the midlands and right up the east coast overnight, before reaching the finish in Bangor on Easter Tuesday.'

'Boy, that's a long way. Would you not be better off starting right away if you have that length to go?' was the logical response!

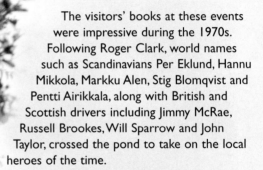

The visitors' books at these events were impressive during the 1970s. Following Roger Clark, world names such as Scandinavians Per Eklund, Hannu Mikkola, Markku Alen, Stig Blomqvist and Pentti Airikkala, along with British and Scottish drivers including Jimmy McRae, Russell Brookes, Will Sparrow and John Taylor, crossed the pond to take on the local heroes of the time.

Not all the visitors were lucky. Peruvian Henri Bradley travelled to Belfast in Cabin 13 from Liverpool, stayed in Room 13 in his Belfast hotel, started at number 13 and retired on the 13th stage of the 1971 Circuit of Ireland. However, in the same year Adrian Boyd won his second Circuit, the 13th in which he had competed, on 13 April!

WAYWARD WARD
Robert Ward's lightweight BMW 2002 goes light on the Knockalla jump in Donegal.

Roger Clark
1960s–70s

From being 'Paddy's Party', the Circuit of Ireland became 'Roger's Romp' in 1968, 1969 and 1970, when the Leicestershire lad, accompanied by Jim Porter, took three consecutive victories. And 'Roger's Romps' were always quite a party, as I would find out many years later when I was locked in a bar in Donegal overnight with the rallying legend!

TON UP OVER TORR
Roger Clark on the Torr Head stage in County Antrim on the 1975 Circuit, in a fuel-injected BDA Mark I

HAPPY HAT TRICK
Roger Clark and Jim Porter recorded three Circuit wins in a row. In 1970 they used this RS1600 Mark I Escort.

Although he drove a Renault Dauphine, Minis and Cortinas in Ireland, Roger Clark will always be associated with the Ford Escort. His first Circuit of Ireland win was highly significant because it was also the first outing for the Escort Twin-Cam and effectively the end of the Mini era.

Roger's two RAC Rally wins in 1972 and 1976 are his most famous, but we witnessed his spectacular sideways style on many occasions on these shores, and his mischievous grin whenever there was a bit of fun to be had. In addition to his three Circuit wins he was also victorious in Galway in 1977.

Cahal Curley

1970s

There's a twinkle in Cahal's eye that would blind you, and his driving in the 1970s was as sparkling as his personality. The Fermanagh car salesman ducked and dived to secure the finance for the Escorts and Porsches that were the 'must have' machines in their day, and he became 'Mr Donegal' when his name was etched on the first three trophies of the Donegal International Rally in 1972, 1973 and 1974.

MILK MAKETH THE MAN
Teetotaller Cahal Curley celebrates with a bottle of milk in 1974.

A FORD IN A FORD
Curley's Ecsort Twin-Cam, in which he won the Northern Ireland Rally Championship, pictured here during the 1971 Circuit of Ireland

DONEGAL DOMINANCE
Curley's Porsche Carrera on its way
to victory in Donegal in 1974

31

ANOTHER STRATOSPHERE

The Chequered Flag Lancia Stratos in Donegal in 1975. It would end up on its roof at the feet of owner Graham Warner on the Atlantic Drive stage.

Lancia Stratos
driver Cahal Curley
in 1976

CIGARETTE HANDICAP SYSTEM

Jack Duddy from Gallahers hands over supplies to Cahal Curley and Austin Frazer at the finish of the 1974 Circuit of Ireland. Austin had his own handicap system for his driver. If Cahal drove a good stage he got Benson & Hedges, if it was a poor performance in Austin's estimation, he was handed Park Drive!

Cahal's studious sidekick, Austin Frazer, provided the perfect foil for the teetotalling extrovert, and they added the Circuit of Ireland and Manx International rallies in 1974 to their list of victories, to the considerable jubilation of their large band of followers, which included songwriter Phil Coulter.

Cahal's association with Graham Warner's Chequered Flag Organisation brought him runs in their Porsches and in the sensational Lancia Stratos. Cahal was always in the top times and often in the number one spot, but the song that Phil dedicated to his rallying hero never made the top ten!

The Curley followers were well organised. They followed CB, as he is known, around in a mini-van, and when they hit town, each one had a specific task. The 'Catering Manager' organised the food, the 'Accommodation Manager' the beds, and the 'Entertainments Manager' got the piano positioned for the entertainer. As the entertainer was no less a person than Phil Coulter, the party was guaranteed.

Adrian Boyd
1960s–70s

Bespectacled and slight, Adrian was an unlikely hero, but that's exactly what he became overnight when, at the age of nineteen, he won the top event in the country.

The son of a Carnmoney quarry owner was unknown before Easter 1960, but with Maurice Johnston working miracles on the maps and Adrian tweaking the handbrake of their 'Frogeyed Sprite' to great effect, they lifted that year's UAC trophy.

ADRIAN ATTACKS
Adrian Boyd climbs the Tim Healey Pass in the Lombard and Ulster MK1 Escort on the 1973 Circuit.

IRISH FIRST

Adrian Boyd (left), partnered by John Davenport, became the first Irish driver to win the Manx International Rally in 1973.

Adrian Boyd, like Paddy Hopkirk, became a household name. In addition to his numerous successes at home and in the UK – which included second and third places in the RAC Rally Championship in 1971 and 1973 – he drove in classic Continental events such as the Spa–Sofia–Liège in 1964 using a semi-works Humber Sceptre, the Monte Carlo Rally in 1968 in a works Hillman Imp, and he was fourth on the Austrian Alpine Rally in 1970 in his own Mark I Escort.

WIDE LOAD

The works Rootes line-up for the 1964 Circuit: mechanic Jim Martin (first from left); Adrian Boyd (second from left) and Beatty Crawford (second from right) with the Humber Super Snipe that would prove too wide for the Kerry roads; Charles Eyre-Maunsell (in trilby) and Alex Spence (first from right) had the more nimble Sunbeam Alpine.

35

UNDERPOWERED PLASTIC
Adrian Boyd's Renault Alpine A110 (seen on the 1975 Circuit) suffered from having a standard Renault 16 engine.

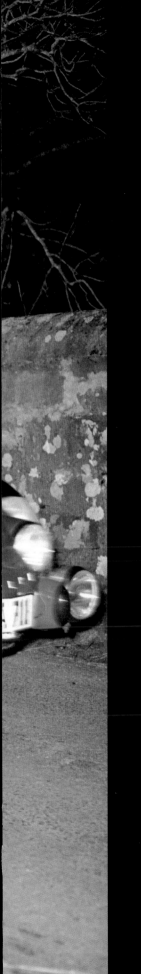

ULSTER ASSAULT

Derek Boyd won the Ulster International Rally in 1977 in the Esler Crawford Photography Porsche Carrera (now owned by Esler Crawford).

Adrian came close to Ireland's top prize again in 1967 and 1968, when he was runner-up on the Circuit in a Cooper S, registration number JBL 494D. Indeed, he used the same car and the same co-driver – Beatty Crawford – to come third in the Easter classic in 1969. Adrian would have to wait eleven years before he would hold the UAC trophy aloft again. In the intervening years he, Cahal Curley and Billy Coleman became the top trio in Irish rallying.

Sponsorship had made its mark by the 1970s, and Lombard & Ulster's backing for the RE Hamilton Team that Adrian drove for brought with it a new style of promotion and high jinks. Adrian, with the experienced John Davenport in the passenger seat, beat his arch rival Cahal Curley on the Isle of Man in 1973 to become the first Irishman to win the Manx Trophy.

As Adrian was hitting the headlines, his younger brother Derek was also notching up some excellent results. Derek Boyd's big weekend came in 1977 when he beat the works Vauxhalls to win the Ulster International in his privately owned Porsche Carrera. He also drove Triumph TR7s for the works team.

THREE YEARS IN THE TOP THREE

Adrian Boyd and Beatty Crawford in JBL 494D at the start of the 1968 Circuit of Ireland. They reached a top-three placing in this Cooper S on the 1967, 1968 and 1969 Circuits.

Ronnie
McCartney

Ronnie, the eldest of the brothers McCartney from Omagh, was in many ways the 'Del Boy' of Irish motorsport, except that, unlike his fictional TV mate from Peckham, he operated completely above board. Ronnie could not go out the door without buying something, and it was often a rally car.

OIL BURNER
It took thirty-seven gallons of oil to get Ronnie McCartney and Terry Harryman home on the 1964 Circuit.

PORSCHE POWER
Ronnie McCartney made it a Porsche one-two on the 1974 Circuit when he finished behind Cahal Curley.

In a very illustrious competition career, Ronnie, who did not believe in hiding his light under a bushel, had two massive highlights. The first was his Circuit of Ireland win with Terry Harryman in 1964, when he virtually carried his Mini across the finish line.

There were victories for both McCartney brothers in Galway, and Ronnie, who was particularly useful on loose surfaces, won his home event, the Bushwhacker Rally, held in the hills above Omagh, many times. But it was twenty-seven years after his Circuit triumph that Ronnie would once again enjoy a major victory in a Mini. This time it was in Beatty Crawford's Cooper S, and the jubilant pair posed against a backdrop of the Dolomites with their trophies for the 1991 Pirelli Classic Marathon.

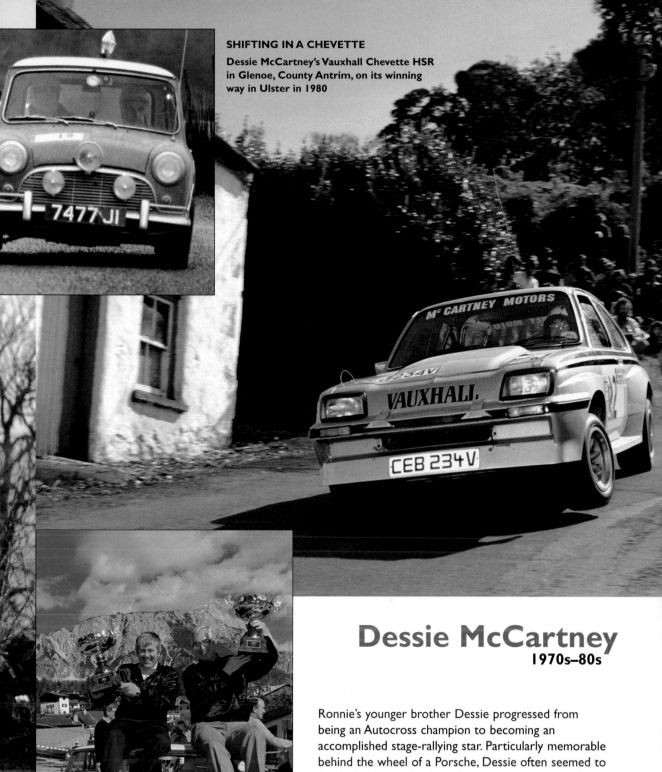

SHIFTING IN A CHEVETTE

Dessie McCartney's Vauxhall Chevette HSR in Glenoe, County Antrim, on its winning way in Ulster in 1980

Dessie McCartney
1970s–80s

Ronnie's younger brother Dessie progressed from being an Autocross champion to becoming an accomplished stage-rallying star. Particularly memorable behind the wheel of a Porsche, Dessie often seemed to be the 'bridesmaid', taking the runner-up spot on the Circuit of Ireland, Manx International and Donegal International rallies. That elusive Irish international win finally came in Galway in 1975, when the younger McCartney powered his Carrera to victory in front of David Agnew's and Jack Tordoff's similar cars. He also won the Ulster International Rally in 1980.

MARATHON MOMENT

Ronnie McCartney (left) and Beatty Crawford win the 1991 Pirelli Classic Marathon.

39

Billy Coleman

1970s–80s

CAMERA SHY
Billy was never comfortable in the limelight.
He's pictured here in Galway in 1978 with the
Chequered Flag Stratos.

He's the classic Irish anti-hero. Shy, self-effacing, yet cunning and quietly charismatic. It is therefore no surprise that Billy travelled the length of the country and stood quietly at the back as his hero, Joey Dunlop, was laid to rest in July 2000.

BUNGEE CORD SPECIAL
TIU 250 was mechanically much more sophisticated than it appeared when Billy drove it in the 1973 Donegal International Rally.

There was intense rivalry between Dealer Opel Team Ireland team-mates Billy Coleman and Austin McHale, especially when Billy snatched victory from the Dublin driver in the dying stages of the 1984 Circuit of Ireland.

SUPERCAR IN THE SNOW

A short-wheel-based, Ferrari-engined Supercar cannot have been the easiest thing to handle in the 1978 Galway snow.

BUBBLE BATH

Billy Coleman and Ronan Morgan celebrate as winners of the 198... Circuit of Ireland

Make no mistake about it, Billy Coleman is the big name in Irish rallying. Like all the greats in the game he is as good on the loose as he is on the tar, and the roll call of his wins is impressive to say the least: British Rally Champion; Tarmac Rally Champion; fourth overall on the WRC Corsica Rally (a record for an Irish driver); three-times winner of the Circuit, Killarney and Donegal international rallies; and twice winner of the Cork 20 and Galway international rallies.

He has seen two careers. The rallying one started when the shy farmer from Millstreet in County Cork, seeded at number 115, appeared in the tattiest of Escorts on the 1969 Circuit of Ireland and proceeded to challenge for third place. He went on to win the British Championship in the Thomas Motors Mark I Escort five years later, but when all the opportunities seemed to be arriving, he went back to his first love, the farm.

MARK I MAGIC

Billy is heading to his first Circuit win in 1975, with Paul Phelan as passenger.

Ronan Morgan and Dealer Opel Team Ireland prised Billy out of retirement in the 1980s, and he went on to drive for Rothmans in Porsches, a BMW and a Metro 6R4. Billy would admit, in hindsight, that he regrets resisting some of the professional opportunities that were offered to him in motorsport, but in reality he always has been, and always will be, primarily a farmer. His ability behind the wheel was just a God-given talent that he chose to exercise when the notion took him.

METRO MAN

The Cork 20 and Donegal rallies were won by Billy and Ronan Morgan in the Rothmans Metro 6R4 in 1986.

Farming was so much in Billy Coleman's head that he used to ask his co-drivers to use nature references in their pace notes. For example, his notes would say '100 left at conifer, flat over brow at oak'.

TAIL TALKING

Tail-happy in the Rothmans 911 SCRS near Clonmel, County Tipperary, Billy Coleman won the 1985 Donegal and 1986 Galway events in these beautiful but difficult to handle Porsches.

International
invasion

With the Circuit of Ireland and the Ulster Rally often doubling as rounds of the British and Irish championships, the big names were frequently drafted in to compete on our stages. This was a great incentive for local aces, who could compete against world champions on their own tar. But there was one big disincentive for the visitors – local knowledge.

DAWSON'S DAMAGE
Andy Dawson's team had no prior knowledge of the terrain on the 1977 Circuit, and Dawson's Escort shows it!

Pace notes were disliked by the authorities and only allowed in Donegal for a few years after 1975 before being completely banned throughout Ireland. Stage locations were supposed to be secret, but driver reconnaissance was widespread, and cross-dressing and other methods of disguise were not uncommon. One well-known driver in the 1970s was known to use a priest's garb on occasions!

TEMPTING NOTES
The introduction of pace notes helped Achim Warmbold and John Davenport become the first visitors to win the Donegal International Rally in 1975.

TOYOTA TYCOON
Ove Andersson, the Swede who now manages Toyota's rallying and racing competition programme, competing in a Celica on the Circuit in 1977.

Above
TARMAC FIRST
Former National Hunt jockey and Rallycross champion John Taylor became the first Irish Tarmac Rally Champion in 1978.

Right
FAST FINN I
Future World Rally Champion Hannu Mikkola in the works Ford in 1978

Left
PEKKA POWER
Per Eklund in the 350hp Triumph TR7 V8 on the Valentia Island stage of the 1979 Circuit

FAST FINN II

Another future World Champion, Timo Salonen, came to Ireland on two occasions but retired on both. He is seen here in the Fiat 131 Abarth on the Liberty Hall stage of the 1979 Circuit.

Ari Vatanen

1970s–80s

He swept into Ireland, swept the ladies off their feet, and almost swept his Opel Ascona into the Atlantic. Ari's arrival in Donegal in 1975 was nothing short of sensational. Before the rally had started, he had 'roofed' a car on loan from a local dealer, and during the event the Ascona bounced spectacularly from ditch to ditch before its inevitable retirement.

MEPs TOGETHER

Ari Vatanen (left) returned to Ireland in 2000 for the Belfast Millennium Motorsport Festival, where he met fellow Member of the European Parliament John Hume.

BLACK BEAUTY

Ari tosses the famous Escort at the Donegal scenery in 1978.

The dashing, blond Finn had made an indelible impression on the Irish fans, especially the female ones, and he returned to the North-West and to Cork in the famous 'Black Magic' Escort.

The most memorable performance on these shores from the future World Champion was in 1980 when he and Jimmy McRae battled for five days on the Circuit of Ireland before 'Ari Vat, the reckless rat', as the rhyme of the time christened him, hit the bank once too often in his efforts to stay with the Vauxhall driver.

Terry Harryman was Ari's other Irish connection. Terry co-drove the handsome Finn in the Peugeot T16 to wins on the 1,000 Lakes, San Remo, RAC, Monte Carlo and Swedish World Championship events in 1984 and 1985, but when they both nearly perished on the 1985 Argentinian event, their friendship cooled.

THE ULTIMATE ESCORT

Ari in 'Black Magic' in its final form on the 1982 Circuit of Ireland

ROTHMANS ROOFED

Ari had to settle for second place on the 1980 Circuit, when he roofed his Escort on the final night of his five-day epic battle with Jimmy McRae.

'The Finns and the Irish have a lot in common, similar sense of humour, they love rallying, that's why I love coming here,' Ari told me many years later. Of all the visiting superstars – and we have seen virtually all of them in action over the years – Ari Vatanen and Henri Toivonen were the most loved.

Pentti Airikkala
1970s–80s

The Finn Pentti Airikkala is still the only driver from outside Britain and Ireland to have won the Circuit of Ireland, in 1979.

The circumstances in which he won the Circuit were most bizarre: the Ulster Automobile Club were brave enough – or foolish enough – to start their Easter classic in the middle of a petrol crisis, and during a phone strike. Remember, there were no mobile phones in those days.

The rally ground to a halt in Galway when the cars ran out of fuel, and it was suspended until they made their way to Killarney. 'Make your own arrangements' was all the organisers could say. Thankfully, regular supplies were replenished in Kerry, and Pentti returned to Belfast in his Chevette HS as the winner.

PETROL REPLENISHED

Pentti on the Sunday Run at Caragh Lake during the 1979 Circuit

Tony Pond

1970s–80s

Four-times Manx International winner Tony Pond was undoubtedly one of the fastest drivers of all time on tarmac, but his luck seldom held in Ireland.

The British driver's biggest triumph on Irish shores was his victory in Lurgan Park in 1991 driving a Metro 6R4, the type of car that he first drove in Donegal in 1985.

TERRIFIC TONY
Tony Pond led the 1981 Circuit of Ireland in this works Vauxhall Chevette HSR until his gearbox failed on the second day.

53

Henri Toivonen

Henri came from a motor sporting family. His father, Pauli, was European Rally Champion and winner of the Monte Carlo Rally, and his brother Harri was a competitor in rallying and long-distance sports car racing.

His visits to Ireland with the Rothmans Team proved to be painful experiences. In 1982, driving an Opel Ascona, he sprained his wrist on a jump; in 1984 the team returned with their Porsche 911s – this time Henri hurt his back in a karting publicity run in Waterford.

Henri was a startling young talent. He had taken his first RAC Rally win at just twenty-four in a Sunbeam Lotus. He had many fans in Ireland, and his tragic death in the Lancia Delta S4 on the 1986 Tour de Corse brought not only his and co-driver Sergio Cresto's lives to a close, but it also led to the Group B Supercars being banished.

HIGHBORN HENRI
They did not come any braver then Henri Toivonen. Here the Finn is flying on the 1984 Circuit.

Mark
Lovell
1980s

TEA TIME
Terry Harryman
(left), Ford Chief
Engineer Gordon
Spooner (centre)
and Mark Lovell
brew up on the 1988
Cork 20 Rally.

Mark had a mighty drive on
the 1986 Circuit of Ireland in
the Group B Ford RS200, when
he followed home Russell
Brookes and winner Dai
Llewellin's Metro 6R4.

Lovell really made his mark in Irish rallying
in 1987 and 1988, driving a Ford of
Ireland–backed Group A Sierra Cosworth.
Usually accompanied by
Ronan Morgan, the
Englishman took
consecutive Tarmac
crowns and won six
qualifying events, as Irish
rallying recovered from
the void left by the
banished Supercars.

TURBO TURMOIL
Mark Lovell catches
his wayward Sierra
on the 1988 Ulster
International Rally.

Local
honour

PORSCHE POWER

Brian Nelson (left) and Malcom Neill line up in their familiar 911, though it was with a David Sutton Escort that they became Tarmac champions.

Ger
Buckley
1970s

IN THE FAMILY

Billy Coleman's cousin Ger Buckley, from County Cork, in his Vauxhall HSR on the 1981 Donegal rally. The five-times winner of the Cork 20 was runner-up in the Tarmac Championship in 1981.

Brian Nelson is the only Irish driver to have achieved top honours in both racing and rallying in this country. Following a circuit-racing career in which the Hillsborough driver was a Formula Libre Champion in Ireland and Scotland, an American Formula B Champion and competed against such notables as five-times Grand Prix winner John Watson, Brian transferred to rallying in the 1970s, taking two Donegal International wins and becoming the Irish Tarmac Rally Champion in 1979.

Brian
Nelson

1970s

AIR LIFT
Brian Nelson bouncing his BMW in Donegal

The multiple Autotest champion entered rallying with a gang of devoted followers from Castlederg at the height of the Group 1 wars. Dominated by Escort RS2000s, this category for production cars spawned intense competition between the locals and the many visitors from Britain and further afield, but John was a match for any visitor.

John Lyons
1970s–80s

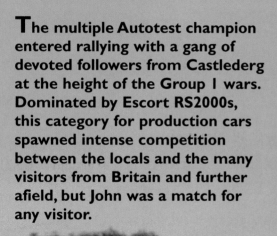

RADIO AHEAD

John Lyons in the Downtown Radio Escort on course for his first International win in Donegal in 1981

The 'giant-killer' often seemed to perform way above the ability of his machinery. His win on the 1978 Donegal Rally stands out among the many memorable moments from this exhilarating driver. With one stage to go, John seemed to have rolled his lead away, but he righted the wreck and took thirty-seven seconds off a surprised Sean Campbell. He graduated to Group 2 machinery with an Opel Kadett and eventually to a Group 4 Escort, in which he won the 1981 and 1982 Donegal international rallies.

HEDGE HOPPER

Lyons, in the Group 1 Escort, was always close to the edge!

Jimmy McRae

1980s

The Circuit of Ireland became the 'Mc Circuit' in the 1980s and 90s, when the McRae family from Lanark, Scotland, won the Easter classic eight times in twelve attempts! Colin McRae, later the first World Rally Champion from the UK, completed the family joy by winning the Circuit in 1991, but it was his quiet-spoken father, Jimmy, who really put the family name in the Circuit record books.

EPIC WEEKEND
Jimmy's Chevette HSR heads home over Torr Head having finally beaten Ari Vatanen to take his first Circuit win in 1980.

Jimmy, a late starter in the sport at the age of thirty, chalked up seven victories on the event that was always regarded as the toughest in the English and Irish championships.

The five times British Rally Champion had become a naturalised Irishman to the fans, as in addition to his record number of Circuit of Ireland wins, Jimmy also won the Irish Tarmac Rally Championship in 1980 and 1981.

BRUT NEVER TASTED BETTER
Jimmy McRae and Mike Nicholson with the bubbly at Belfast City Hall in 1980

THE MULTITUDES AT MOLL'S
Early morning at Moll's Gap in 1980

METRO MOUNTAINEERING
Jimmy in the Rothmans Metro 6R4, which led the 1986 Circuit of Ireland until it had a cam-belt failure.

NOT IN 1989

Jimmy McRae won in Ulster
in 1981, 1986 and 1987, but
1989 (seen here) was
Gwyndaf Evans's year.

THREE IN A ROW

Jimmy opened his 1980s Circuit account with three consecutive wins. This is the car in which he got the Easter hat trick in 1982.

FOUR UP

Cutting it close on the 1985 Circuit. Jimmy is on his way to his fourth Circuit win in car number 4, the Manta 400.

BENT BUT NOT BEATEN
Damaged on the first stage, the Andrews Heat for Hire
Escort made an amazing recovery to win the 1978 Circuit.

Russell
Brookes

1970s–80s

MANTA MAGIC

Russell Brookes and Mike Broad on their way to
victory on the 1985 Ulster Rally

'Little Legs' was one of the top names to
emerge from the British Ford Mexico rally
championships in the 1970s, and he first
appeared on the Circuit of Ireland in one of
these 1600cc Group 1 Escorts in 1974. The
Birmingham boy liked the Irish tarmac, and
he returned that same year in an RS2000 to
win his class in Donegal and on the Texaco
Rally (the forerunner to the Ulster Rally).

By 1977 Russell had graduated to Group 4 cars, and he won
his first of three Circuits that year. Russell also had wins in
Ulster and West Cork, and the twice British Rally Champion
was victorious on the Isle of Man on three occasions. He
was runner-up in the 1982 and 1983 Irish Tarmac
championships and clinched the top spot in 1989.

The rivalry between Brookes and McRae has always been
intense, and Jimmy, I suspect, has found the relationship
difficult at times.

Super
cars

The term Supercar is somewhat unfairly linked to certain 1980s designs, as there have been outstanding machines in every era. In the 1970s there were the Austin Healey 3000s, Alpine A110s, Porsche 911s and the daddy of them all, the Ferrari-engined Lancia Stratos.

But when the chattering waste-gate of the Audi Quattro exploded on the scene in 1981 it became the Supercar that changed the face of stage rallying for all time. Its turbo-charged four-wheel-drive configuration was a little fragile in its original Group 4 form, but with the introduction of the more flexible Group B rules, the Quattro initially led the pack for the short-lived period between 1982 and 1986, which has historically become known as the Supercar era.

Under the Group 4 regulations, manufacturers had to produce a minimum of four hundred cars similar to their rallying machines per year to have them approved for competition. The Group B rules reduced that number to two hundred per year, and the floodgates in the design offices burst open, spewing out such sensational all-wheel-drive machines as the A1, A2, Sport and E2 from Audi; the 037 Rally and S4 Delta from Lancia; the RS200 from Ford; the Metro 6R4 from Austin Rover; and the most successful of all, the Peugeot 205 T16.

WHISPERING GIANT
Stig Blomqvist in the 370bhp A1 Audi Quattro on the 1983 Circuit. He brought the car back to win the 1983 Ulster International Rally.

All, with the exception of the S4 Delta, were seen in action on the Irish stages, and although their two-wheel-drive brothers struggled internationally, it was often a different story on the bumpy Irish roads, where the less sophisticated Manta 400s and Porsche 911 SCRSs would often outlast their exotic opposition.

FLAME SPITTING

Note the flames from the over-run out of Mikael Sundstrom's 350bhp Peugeot T16 during the 1985 Ulster Rally

FORD'S SUPERCAR
Mark Lovell in the 420bhp Ford RS200 on the 1986 Circuit

LUSCIOUS LANCIA

Two of the Lancia Rally 037s were seen in Ireland: this 325bhp
car was driven by Pentti Airikkala in the 1983 Circuit of Ireland;
Dessie McCartney had a much milder version.

FLYING FRENCHMAN
Bernard Beguin in the Flat 6 300bhp Rothmans Porsche 911 SCRS
during the 1985 Circuit of Ireland

Happily, Rothmans major involvement in the sport coincided with the Supercar era, and their professional promotion, as well as the presence of superstars such as Hannu Mikkola, Stig Blomqvist, Walter Röhrl, Henri Toivonen, Michèle Mouton, Malcolm Wilson, Pentti Airikkala, Jimmy McRae, Russell Brookes, Mark Lovell, Tony Pond, Dai Llewellin and Mikael Sundstrom, made the 1980s the golden years on Irish tarmac.

ONE OFF

Walter Röhrl, the Bishop's Secretary who
became twice World Champion, came
once to Ireland and won.

Walter Röhrl 1980s

The tall, sombre German seemed to win the
1984 Ulster International Rally with calculated
ease. Admittedly, he had the awesome 510hp
Audi Quattro Sport at his disposal, but he
certainly had no prior knowledge of the stages.
On his one and only competitive visit to Ireland
he definitely impressed.

ON A RÖHRL

The Short Quattro on the 1984
Ulster Rally

Dai
Llewellin

1980s–90s

DAI-NAMIC
Dai Llewellin gave the six-cylinder V6 Metro
6R4 its first international win on the 1986
Circuit of Ireland.

Bertie Fisher

1980s–90s

EARLY DAYS
Bertie in the Group 1 Escort RS2000
on the Fanad stage in Donegal

For all Bertie's ability to arrive on time, and ahead of most at the end of stages, he was a notoriously bad timekeeper in everyday life. Team manager Sydney Meeke used to tell him a meeting was at ten o'clock when it was really at eleven, and Bertie would still often be late.

'Ballinamallard Bertie' I used to call him, and on reflection it is an apt title, as the Fisher family are the lifeblood of the Fermanagh village. Bertie not only catapulted to success on the stages, but he and his brother Ernie also led the family firm of structural engineers to become the major employer in the area and one of the most respected companies in the UK construction industry.

Bertie was a fair employer and an ultra-fair competitor. His four Irish Tarmac Rally titles and record number of twenty Tarmac wins only tell a little of the story. He was a sports ambassador. He cared about safety so deeply that he retired from competition during the insurance crisis of the 1980s and volunteered his services as a safety officer. Only when he felt sufficiently at ease with the situation did he return to his driving role.

The Fisher rallying family consisted of others that were as close as kin. Fellow Fermanagh man Austin Frazer, after Cahal Curley retired, accompanied Bertie on many successful outings before Donegal's Rory Kennedy took over as his regular co-driver in the 1990s. Sydney Meeke prepared all Bertie's early cars, and even when Prodrive took over, Sydney

FISHER FAMILY

Top: Bertie with his wife, Gladys, and daughter, Emma

Left: Bertie with his father, Tommy

FIRST FIRST
Bertie Fisher's first international win, partnered by Austin Frazer, on the 1982 Ulster Rally

FULL OF THE RACK
Bertie and co-driver Austin Frazer in
a customary pose on the 1980
Circuit of Ireland

always kept a watchful eye. In the latter years no Fisher outing would have been complete without the presence of 'Big Mac', Kieran McAnallan, Bertie's long-time sponsor and friend.

Bertie had high hopes that his talented son Mark would achieve the world championship status in the sport that he had never had the opportunity to attain. That plan was very much on course when a tragic helicopter accident took Bertie, his daughter, Emma, and Mark from us in 2001. It is a blow from which the sport will never fully recover.

HAPPY DAYS
From left: Rory Kennedy (co-driver), Mark Fisher, Sydney Meeke (team manager) and Bertie Fisher

SOLID GOLD
Bertie in the Gold Card Manta 400 which led the 1984 Circuit of Ireland

The arrival of Bertie Fisher's Subaru Impreza on Irish shores in 1994 certainly impressed one fan in Killarney.

'Did you see her, Plum? The Imprezzza! There she was at the start of a stage, and her like a tethered-down buck rabbit, and her mad for road!'

TOUGH ACTION

A tough test in the Toughmac Impreza in Donegal before the 1998 Circuit of Ireland

Austin
McHale

1980s–present

DEALER OPEL TEAM IRELAND

Austin McHale

Rothmans Circuit of Ireland Rally

10

Shell Oils

fordrallyesport

McHALE DYNASTY

The three rallying McHales, Aaron (left), Austin and Gareth, during the 2004 Donegal rally.

Rugged, sometimes gruff, quizzical and often slightly intimidating – that is Austin, the man with the never-say-die attitude that has brought him right to the top of the record books in Irish rallying. Fisher, Coleman and McHale have been the undisputed top Irish trio of the modern era, and when it comes to Tarmac championships, Austin holds the record.

SO CLOSE

Austin's first Circuit of Ireland win seemed to be on the cards in 1984 when the rally came out of Donegal on the final morning, but a last-minute engine failure robbed him of victory.

Austin used a Group A Opel Monza on the 1987 Circuit of Ireland. It had a heavy tailgate that contained an equally heavy rear window. After the first few stages the tailgate fell out, and Austin and Christy Farrell had a draughty but swifter ride round Ireland until a 'replacement' was found just minutes before the final scrutiny!

AGAVANAGH JUMP

The Celica comes down to earth on the 1997 Circuit. A year
later Austin put up a sensational late charge to beat Bertie
Fisher and take his second Circuit win.

REAR-ENDED

Austin's Celica does not look 'tail happy'
in Donegal in 1992.

Originally from Mayo but now running a highly successful contracting business in Dublin, Austin has been Tarmac Champion five times. His progress through the ranks to the world rally cars has always been spectacular and thrilling to watch. Like Fisher, he is creating a rallying dynasty, with his sons, Aaron and Gareth, competing with increasing success. Indeed, one wonders if Austin would have retained the motivation to continue for such a long time had it not been for Fisher, his arch rival and friend.

Like Coleman, we first took notice of Austin in a tatty black Ford, particularly when his Group 1 Escort took third place in the snow-covered forestry stages of Yorkshire during a British Championship round. He gained his first Tarmac Championship title driving a Vauxhall Chevette HSR in 1983, but the fireworks really began when he came up against Billy Coleman, his team-mate of the time in Dealer Team Opel Ireland, during the 1984 season.

VAUXHALL DAYS
Austin's Team PR Reilly Chevette HSR in third place on the 1982 Circuit. This car would bring him his first Tarmac title a year later.

VIDEO ACTION
The Xtra-vision BMW M3 on a run to glory in Galway
in 1991, on a rally that Austin has won six times.

Austin had set up the DTOI deal and felt that Billy had been squeezed in on the act with pressure from the southern dealers, so when Billy took the Circuit win and the Tarmac title in 1984 it did not help the relationship.

The Manta was re-sprayed in Shell's black livery for the 1985 and 1986 seasons, and Austin took the title on both occasions. He repeated the title double in 1997 and 1998 for Toyota, but the record number of Irish Tarmac rally wins is still held by the late Bertie Fisher, and beating that must still be a target for the Dubliner.

TROUBLED TIMES

The same tight team have looked after Austin's rally cars for years. Here he gets a little roadside assistance in Killarney in 1998.

A FAMILY AFFAIR
Wherever Frank went,
his parents, Mary and
Leo, went too.

Frank
Meagher 1980s–90s

ALWAYS THE UNDERDOG
Frank Meagher, the underdog, led the works
Ford Cosworths in Galway and Cork in 1989!

Irish sporting heroes seem to come in two extremes, the shy Billy Coleman type or the extrovert Eddie Irvine style. Frank was in the former camp and, like Billy, he was a god in his own land. In the shadows of Slievenamon in County Tipperary, he learnt to slide cars on the Carrick-on-Suir Motor Club's forestry events, and it is a tragic irony that he lost his life in a private test in the same area.

CIRCUIT WINNER
The Cosworth in which Frank won the 1992 Circuit is pictured in Donegal.

Frank's Galway International drive in 1989, when he led the Ford Motor Company's Sierra Cosworth (driven by Mark Lovell) by four minutes, and his Cork 20 outing in the same year are now part of Irish rallying history. In Cork he was ahead of Saeed Al Hajri in the David Sutton–prepared Cosworth, before mechanical maladies, as in Galway, brought his home-prepared Mark II Escort to a premature halt.

But Frank will be remembered most as a driver who made huge sacrifices to beat the financial odds, and beat them he well and truly did. With the Irish National Rally title in the bag, Frank moved on to the International scene and won the Circuit of Ireland, and nearly the Tarmac Championship, in 1992. Three years later, when the coffers had been replenished once again, he took the country's top rallying award, having won Galway, Killarney, the Manx International and Cork 20 rallies along the way.

Everywhere Frank went the family went too. Initially it was just his parents, Mary and Leo, but later his wife, Ronnie, and the kids were always at the party. When the champagne sprayed there was a young Meagher in one arm and a trophy in the other. And the family involvement did not end there. Tom Gahan, Frank's brother-in-law, looked after the cars, and Pat Moloughney, another family member, often called the notes when Frank's usual co-driver, Michael Maher (no relation), was not around.

WET IN THE NORTH-WEST

Frank loved the ex-Kankkunen WRC Escort Cosworth
that he rallied in 1999.

RPM TV reporter Gary
Gillespie said to Frank
in Cork in 1989: 'What
could you do with a
works car?'

Frank blinked and
replied: 'Take her handy
and win every event
around!'

James
Cullen
1980s–present

'Talent in abundance but money in short supply.' It could be the title of the Irish rallyman's anthem, and it certainly applies to Letterkenny's James Cullen. In fact, if it had not been for faithful supporters like Tony Kelly and Frank Grimes, James would never have made it into this book.

James started out in the rallying game as Clerk of the Course of his own county's international event, but the urge to get behind the wheel was great; and the minute that he did, his talent was transparent. After years of struggle the emotions overflowed when he and co-driver Ellen Morgan stood on the bonnet of their pink Sierra Cosworth in 1991, as winners of the Donegal International Rally.

A Group N Tarmac title was attained in 1993, but there was never the budget to do a full year at the highest level. One further moment of international glory would come in 1999, when James and Ellen once again won Donegal, this time in a Subaru Impreza.

MONSTERING IT OVER MUCKISH
James led Lovell in Donegal in his 'old'
Ascona 400 in 1988.

QUESTION TIME
James gets a grilling from 'Plum' Tyndall and the *RPM* TV team.

IN THE PINK
James and Ellen's first Donegal International win in 1991

DONEGAL DRIFTERS

James and Ellen in the Group A Escort Cosworth
on the Inishowen Peninsula in 1998

A new generation of
Supercars

COLIN IN CONSULTATION

Future World Rally Champion Colin McRae receives a few words of advice from Sammy Hamill, the doyen of Irish motorsports journalism, during the 1989 Ulster Rally.

The presence of professional drivers on Irish stages has undoubtedly raised the level of local driving talent over the years, and the early 1990s were no exception. While Jimmy McRae's career was on the wane, his sons Colin and Alister were just reaching their peak. Like others, they came to Ireland as part of the British Championship package. With Colin came two other future world champions, Tommi Makinen and Richard Burns.

LASHING THE LEGACY

Colin McRae in typically exuberant style on his way to winning the Ulster Rally in 1992

TOP GUN

Malcolm Wilson, the 1993 Ulster Rally
winner, drove and prepared the Michelin
Pilot Escort Cosworths.

CHAMPIONS CHAT
Future British and world rally champions Gwyndaf Evans (left) and Richard Burns chat during the 1993 Ulster Rally.

YOU CAN IN A NISSAN
Tommi Makinen leaping over the Ulster terrain in the Formula 2 Nissan in 1994

SUPER SEAT

The Ulster Rally has been good to Gwyndaf
Evans: he won his first International there in
1989, but here he is seen in the Kit Car
SEAT on the 1998 event.

Mechanical
miracles

Rally cars are built to be worked on. Side windows and panels are made to be removed, fly nuts replace the more conventional type, and nuts and bolts never have time to rust. Where possible everything is accessible. Transmissions lie pre-assembled in the service vans for quick replacement, but this does not take away from the miracles that are performed by the teams in service areas.

AN POST AT YOUR SERVICE
Henri Toivonen's Ascona is fitted with a new gearbox outside a County Tipperary post office during the 1982 Circuit.

The highly skilled mechanics work against time; in most instances they will have only twenty minutes to undertake the normal maintenance tasks, let alone mechanical or accident repairs. They work in all weathers and in all light conditions, wrestling with hot exhausts and turbos in order to beat the clock. And in between the frantic work periods, there are those long, cold and boring waits, often miles from the action that is thrilling the fans.

Jobs that literally take days in a local garage are performed in minutes, and with modern computerised technology it would seem at times that engines are self-healing!

SERVICING TIPS
There's no time to use a jack on Ronnie McCartney's Escort on the 1979 Circuit. A new drive shaft, ferried over to Valentia Island, is fitted on the spot.

ALL HANDS ON DECK

Sydney Meeke and the Prodrive men descend on Bertie Fisher's Subaru Legacy during the 1993 Donegal rally.

Eamon Boland in reply to an *RPM* TV reporter on the 2003 Ulster International Rally who is marvelling at the speed at which the Dom Buckley mechanics have changed a gearbox on his Subaru: 'Don't tell anyone,' jokes Eamon, 'or all our garage customers will want the same service.'

SERVICE PANIC

The race against the clock to refettle Austin McHale and Brian Murphy's car in Omagh during the 2004 Circuit

Kenny
McKinstry

1980s–present

Kenny's commitment to rallying can never be questioned. His modest home in Banbridge, dwarfed by the modern McKinstry Motorsport workshops in the backyard, is physical proof of where the McKinstry family's priorities lie.

GROUP I GROUPIE

Like most of our top drivers, Kenny McKinstry, pictured here on the Ballaghbeama Pass in 1981, learnt his stage skills in Group I (now Group N).

KING KENNY
Kenny McKinstry and Robbie Philpott fly high on the 1992 Donegal Rally. They won the Tarmac Championship in this car two years later.

Kenny McKinstry, twice Tarmac Champion

Kenny came up through the ranks. From night navigation events he moved on to Group 1 and then Group 4 categories, and he made the Lurgan Park event his own, having won the North Armagh Motor Club's lucrative event a record ten times.

His partnership with the commercially minded Robbie Philpott brought good sponsorship from Kaliber in the 1990s. This enabled Kenny and Robbie to take the Tarmac Group N title in 1991 and, by a quirk of fate, the overall Tarmac title in the same year. With the Kaliber money they bought a Subaru Legacy, and when Stephen Finlay faltered in 1994, Kenny took his second Tarmac crown.

Kenny, who now concentrates on his rally-hire business, has won the Galway and Cork 20 international rallies twice, and his British National Rally Championship win in 1999 shows his versatility on both tarmac and loose surfaces.

Stephen Finlay

1980s–90s

Unlike many in motorsport, Stephen had both the ability and the means to rally at the highest level. There was just one snag – he hated the publicity. Like Eamon Boland, he is terminally shy, and he was even suspected of passing up a win on an English event rather than face the podium pomp and the reporters.

TOP PILOT
Stephen Finlay on the 1996 Killarney Rally of the Lakes

From the moment he stepped into a rally car as a teenager, the Ballygawley man was outstandingly quick, but his appearances were sporadic. Business was always a priority, as he had the responsibility of running the family firm from an early age, but whether it was his business commitments or his shyness that prevented him from competing more regularly, we may never know. Whatever the reason, Stephen always returned right at the top of the game, and his mentor, Malcolm Wilson, reckoned he had world-class potential.

His friendship with Malcolm, director of M-Sport, saw him commit to a full Tarmac programme in 1994 in the Michelin Pilot–backed Sierra Cosworth, and but for a disastrous slip on the final round in Cork, he would have been Tarmac Champion. The records show that Stephen won two Circuit of Ireland rallies, one Donegal and one Killarney event, but it seems that he almost had to be cajoled into competing. I wonder whether, when he grows old, he will regret that he did not make more of his talent?

Andrew Nesbitt

1990s–present

Currently there is no one to match the Armagh man's pace on the black stuff. The 2000 and 2002 Tarmac Rally Champion is in a class of his own, and his bravery over the fast sections has been known to terrify even his co-driver, James O'Brien.

DONEGAL DELIGHT
Andrew Nesbitt's first international win in the Donegal Hills in 1996

THE BANANA BUNCH

Andrew (right) and Hannu Mikkola at the Summit 2000 Rally in County Fermanagh

The road to that dominance has not been easy, as in Ireland you first have to make the money before you can make the impact. So when Bertie Fisher and Austin McHale were charging ahead in the Irish rally record books, Andrew seldom had the budget to challenge over a whole season.

The big breakthrough came in Donegal in 1996, when Andrew took his first Tarmac Championship win on the event's twenty-fifth anniversary. It was good for Andrew and good for the sport, as this fun-loving businessman is an outstanding ambassador. He can reel in money at a charity auction as quickly as he and co-driver James O'Brien can shrink the seconds on a special stage.

A frightening road accident in 1998 unsettled him for a season, but we knew that Andrew had really arrived when he swapped times all weekend with the great Bertie Fisher on the 1999 Circuit of Ireland and only conceded victory because of a puncture on the final morning.

BATTLE WITH BERTIE

It was this front puncture that decided the battle between Andrew and Bertie Fisher on the 1999 Circuit.

CIRCUIT GLORY

Andrew on a high on the way to his 2002 Circuit of Ireland win

Following an accident on Atlantic Drive during the 1997 Donegal Rally, Andrew Nesbitt was so keen to get his Celica back on the road that he hot-wired an adjacent tractor in order to pull the Toyota out of the ditch. The farmer was unaware that he had branched out into the tractor-hire business!

On the 2000 Donegal International Rally the Cuisine de France Subaru Impreza created Irish rallying history by taking fastest time on every single stage, and now Andrew's genial handshake and mischievous grin are as likely to be seen at a World Champion round as at an Irish Tarmac Championship event.

**Andrew and Bertie Fisher
at the Summit 2000 Rally**

DIRTY DANCING

**Andrew used the entire road and more on the 2003
Circuit to try to beat Derek McGarrity.**

Beautiful backdrops

Follow the Irish Tarmac Championship and you will be drawn into a wonderland of natural beauty. You could be in the Fermanagh Lakelands at Easter, in the splendour of the Kerry Mountains on the May Bank Holiday weekend, crossing the Hills of Donegal in the early summer, negotiating the lanes of Ulster in September, or exploring the historic city of Cork in the autumn.

The route that the Irish Tarmac Rally Championship takes is not the normal tourist trail. You will not be asked to kiss the Blarney Stone, but you will be led into remote beauty and constantly surprised by magical parts of Ireland that you never even imagined were there.

CONNEMARA

A 'Cossie' in Connemara, with the
Twelve Pins in the background

MALIN HEAD
Eamon Boland crackles through
the Donegal remoteness.

CHASING THE LADIES
Eugene Donnelly powers past
Kilmakilloge Harbour during the
2004 Rally of the Lakes.

THE LADIES WAY

Driver
aids

NO BUNCH OF ROSES
Co-driver Pauline Gullick gets a rough ride with Rosemary Smith in Donegal in 1979.

Some would say that the role of co-drivers, or navigators as they were called in the early days, has diminished over the years. In fact, their role has not so much diminished as changed beyond all recognition.

Navigation in the early days was a battle of wits between the person in the passenger seat and the rally organisers. The route planners did everything in their power to increase the challenge for the competitors, finding obscure roads and tracks in the most remote parts of the country with the aid of rather incomplete Ordnance Survey maps. There were nightmare areas such as the Cavan/Monaghan borders, where lanes were plentiful and mapping was vague.

The situation was further confused by the fact that you could only acquire maps at a scale of one inch to the mile for the Republic, whereas maps for Northern Ireland were available at a scale of one half-inch to the mile.

The early navigator had to 'plot and bash' his way between map reference points and maintain a strict average speed by using stopwatches and average speed charts. His instructions were sometimes recorded as a straightforward list, and sometimes in the form of 'tulip diagrams'. These showed each junction or crossroads as a simplified diagram, with an arrow representing the direction in which you were expected to travel.

Today's co-drivers, as they prefer to be called, have a completely different role. They are primarily responsible for making and calling the pace notes that guide their drivers through the special stages. They have become the

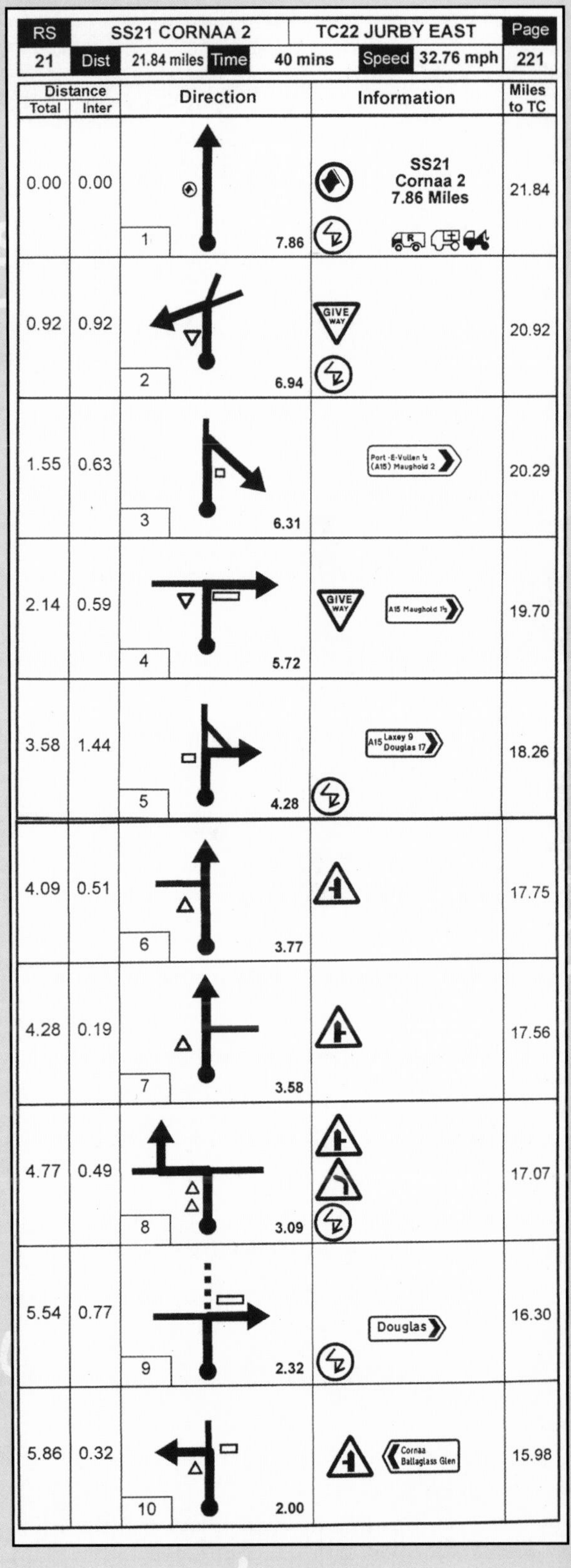

TULIP THEORIES

Explanations for the origin of the term 'tulip diagram' vary: one theory has it that this way of representing a junction was first used on a Tulip Rally in Holland; another claims that the bulb at the base of the stem indicating the direction from which the junction is approached called to mind a tulip.

Tulip diagrams are still an essential aid to rally drivers and co-drivers. The sample shown here is from the road book of the 2004 Manx International Rally, which is one of the Irish Tarmac Championship events.

RS	SS21 CORNAA 2		TC22 JURBY EAST	Page
21	Dist	21.84 miles Time	40 mins Speed 32.76 mph	221

Distance Total	Inter	Direction	Information	Miles to TC
0.00	0.00	1 · 7.86	SS21 Cornaa 2 7.86 Miles	21.84
0.92	0.92	2 · 6.94	GIVE WAY	20.92
1.55	0.63	3 · 6.31	Port ·E·Vullen ½ (A15) Maughold 2	20.29
2.14	0.59	4 · 5.72	GIVE WAY A15 Maughold 1½	19.70
3.58	1.44	5 · 4.28	A15 Laxey 9 Douglas 17	18.26
4.09	0.51	6 · 3.77		17.75
4.28	0.19	7 · 3.58		17.56
4.77	0.49	8 · 3.09		17.07
5.54	0.77	9 · 2.32	Douglas	16.30
5.86	0.32	10 · 2.00	Cornaa Ballaglass Glen	15.98

PONDERING PACENOTES
Ronan Morgan checks his notes on
the 1989 Galway Rally

'office managers' of the whole operation, and a co-driver will often co-ordinate the team's travel, accommodation and service schedules, leaving the driver with as little as possible to do besides driving the rally car.

Pace-noting methods vary enormously from team to team, but there are two basic systems. The descriptive note system, as the title suggests, describes the hazard ahead. For example, '100 flat left over brow, 50 into 90 right, don't cut' means that after 100 metres you go flat out over a brow where the road curves slightly to the left; after 50 metres this is followed by a 90-degree right-hand bend at which you do not cut the corner, as there may be a rock or other object on the inside of the corner.

In a numerical note system, where corners are graded from 1 to 5 according to the speed at which the bend can be taken, instructions for the same section of road would read '100 flat L 5 over brow, into 50 R 2, don't cut'.

All the top teams have their own individual calls. 'Mirage' is a word that is frequently used by James O'Brien, Andrew Nesbitt's co-driver. We think it means deceptive. The word 'maybe' occurs regularly in pace notes, indicating that a decision should be at the driver's discretion, as in 'flat L maybe'.

Down among the amateur co-drivers you will hear some very peculiar calls. 'Hold her flat' and 'Go on ye boy ye!' are among the popular terms of encouragement!

Ireland has produced a number of world-class co-drivers. Terry Harryman's experience spans many eras, from his days at home with Paddy Hopkirk in Minis in the 1950s through to the glory days of the Group B Supercars in the 1980s. Driving with Ari Vatanen, first in the

ME AND LIZ
'Mr and Mrs Rally Bulletin', Brian
and Liz Patterson, have turned rally
information sheets into an art form
over the years. Their commercially
available pace notes are also widely
used in rallying circles.

HEAD HONCHOS

Fred Gallagher (right), pictured here with John Lyons, fulfilled his ambition and became a top World Championship co-driver.

Rothmans Opel Team and later with Peugeot, the Bangor man had six world championship victories before a serious accident in Argentina nearly ended both their careers. Terry was team manager of the Renault Meganes in the British Championship in the Kit Car era, and even now he still accompanies drivers in the Middle East.

Holywood's Fred Gallagher first came to prominence in the motoring world when, as a student, he won the Christmas quiz in *Motoring News*. His rallying career made bigger headlines when he sat with drivers such as Henri Toivonen, Juha Kankkunen and Björn Waldegard. He won two East African Safaris with Juha (1985 and 1986) and a third with Björn some four years later. Fred is now Clerk of the Course of the Rally of Wales, Britain's world championship qualifying event.

Ronan McNamee from Crossmaglen in County Armagh had a World Championship qualifying win with Pentti Airikkala on the 1989 RAC Rally; Dubliner Ronan Morgan has been FIA Middle East Rally Championship Co-Driver many times; Belfast's Bobby Willis has also had many successes in the Middle East and on the desert raids; and Chris Patterson, Rory Kennedy and Gordon Noble regularly accompany drivers on the world rally scene.

The emphasis may have changed, but the importance of the person in the passenger seat is greater than ever. Spare a thought for that co-driver, whom you can hardly see these days, as they now have to virtually sit on the floor to keep the centre of gravity in that World Rally Car as low to the ground as possible. One misjudged time calculation and they could lose the rally for the team, which in turn could cost thousands of pounds. One misread note and they could lose a lot more! Theirs is a brave and highly responsible job.

WRC PARTNERSHIP

Terry Harryman (left) and Ari Vatanen, partners in the Rothmans Opel Team in 1983

EXPERIENCED GUIDE

Gordon Noble (left) guided Mark Fisher to his Tarmac Group N Championship win in 2000.

Historic
inheritance

Historic rallying, to cater for the much-loved cars of the 1960s and 1970s, was introduced in Ireland in the early 1990s. There are two main divisions – the pre-1967 Historic Rally Cars, and the pre-1974 Post-Historic Rally Cars. The Minis, Cortinas, Avengers, Anglias and early Porsches are lovingly cared for and driven by a small but dedicated band, which has regularly included such well-known drivers of the past as Mervyn Johnston and Dessie Nutt, and some equally well-known co-drivers such as Austin Frazer and Beatty Crawford. Billy Coleman, Cahal Curley, Roger Clark and Björn Waldegard have all had guest drives in Irish Historic rallying events.

It's a 'David and Goliath' contest in the Historic category between the Minis and the Porsches, with Dessie Nutt (pictured here at Malin Head) and John Keatley more often than not taking the honours for the German marque, and Mervyn Johnston or Frank Cunningham humbling the Porsche 911s in their magic Minis.

Among the Post-Historic mob, it's usually an Escort/Porsche affair, with the BMW 2002 and Mini also getting a look in. In this category Isle of Man driver Martin Freestone has been the man to beat in his Mark I Escort, but Lloyd Hutchinson has been known to reach indecent speeds in his 1480cc Cooper S.

EVERGREENS

Ernest McMillan (above left) has competed in thirty-two Circuits of Ireland, a dozen Monte Carlos and been involved in over six hundred events. Harry Cathcart cannot be far behind, having competed in so many Circuits, Ulster rallies and Manx Internationals that he has lost count!

The road
ahead

As you read this book, new names will already be featuring in the rally bulletins. This is not only a fast-moving sport but also one with a fast throughput.

As well as Andrew Nesbitt, the men of the moment are Eugene Donnelly, Derek McGarrity, Eamon Boland, Donie O'Sullivan and a newcomer to the international scene, Kevin Lynch. They would be the first to admit that they still have a lot to learn to put themselves on a par with the rallymasters of previous generations.

Will the current Group N chargers like Roy White, the younger McHales, Dessie Keenan and Andrew Stewart become the WRC stars of tomorrow? Will Kris Meeke and Niall McShea make it on the world stage, or might they return to their homeland to entertain us in the future? Only time will tell.

SHOOTING STAR

In just two seasons Kevin Lynch has made a major impact in Irish rallying. The stage novice from Dungiven has uncanny car control on both loose and tarmac surfaces and must have a big future in the sport. He is pictured here during the 2004 Donegal International Rally.

Eamon Boland

This shy driver from Wexford loves nothing more than being behind the wheel of a rally car but nothing less than being in the glare of publicity. He has competed at the highest level for many seasons and was runner-up in the Tarmac Championship on two occasions. He finally achieved that elusive win in Cork in 2003.

Eamon has enormous experience and his car control is magic to watch, but he seems unprepared to risk all on the really fast sections. He has driven Fords, Subarus and Mitsubishis, and in 2002 he finished fifteenth on the Monte Carlo Rally.

MITSUBISHI DEBUT

Eamon Boland, seen here on the 2004 Killarney Rally of the Lakes, was the first privateer to rally a WRC Mitsubishi on Irish soil, and possibly the last. WRC examples of the Mistubishi Lancer are rare, and the team returned to Subarus after two events.

PLAYING MATADOR

Eamon Boland charges an *RPM* cameraman on the 1998 Galway International Rally.

SUBARU SPECIALIST
Although Derek McGarrity trades in every kind of rally car worldwide, his Tarmac success has been in Subarus. Here Derek steers his Subaru WRC S7 round a bend on the Healy Pass during the 2002 Killarney Rally of the Lakes.

Derek
McGarrity

Derek is one of the foremost traders of rally cars in the world, and he usually keeps one of the latest in his catalogue long enough to drive it himself and add to his impressive CV of Tarmac performances – impressive enough to make him Irish Tarmac Rally Champion in 2003. At any time there could be half a dozen WRC cars in his yard at Glengormley, and the one in which he wins is almost certain to be sold as it crosses the finishing line.

Derek is part of an Irish motor sporting dynasty. His father, Patsy, was a multiple motorcycling and motor racing champion, his brother Alan a Formula Ford Champion, and his Uncle Harold and nephew Kevin have all excelled on the race tracks.

Eugene
Donnelly

To say that Eugene is 'mad for road' would be an understatement. The Magherafelt driver covered more rally miles than any other competitor in 2003 when he took the Irish National Rally and Northern Ireland Rally championship titles. He now concentrates on the Tarmac events, and he seems to excel in wet or greasy conditions, when his skill compensates for his Toyota, which has fallen behind a few years in the technology stakes.

This affable 'rally junkie' is as talented as anyone on the Irish stages. He can already give the top men a hard time in early model WRC cars, as he has proved with his Galway (2002) and Killarney (2003) wins, as well as that fabulous race in the 2004 Galway International, when he was defeated by Tapio Laukkunen by only 0.7 of a second!

JOINING THE TARMAC CLUB
Eugene Donnelly joined the club with wins in Galway and Killarney in this Subaru WRC Impreza, pictured here on the 2003 Circuit of Ireland.

Donie
O'Sullivan

Donie follows a long line of successful drivers from the south-west of Ireland who have been inspired to take up rallying by the visits of the Circuit of Ireland at Easter and, more recently, the Killarney Rally of the Lakes in spring.

His enthusiastic approach to life is reflected in his driving style. When you watch the in-car footage of the Killarney driver's bravery as his car skates over the treacherous surfaces, it can be as frightening as watching Andrew Nesbitt's wild action on the same sections.

LOCAL HERO

Moll's Gap during the 2004 Killarney Rally of the Lakes, and the crowds are out in force to support their local charger. It was to be an unlucky event for Donie, though, as he rolled out of his impressive second position.

Finishing lines

The two great masters of the Irish Tarmac Championship have undoubtedly been Bertie Fisher and Austin McHale. Their friendly rivalry fuelled their contests over a quarter of a century, and they stuck with the series more consistently than many others. The length of time they spent on the tarmac trail should in no way detract from their achievements: these two gifted amateurs, who largely financed their years of competition from their own resources, were more than fit for their professional contemporaries when they came to visit. At the time of writing it seems appropriate that they share the spoils in the record books. Austin has been Tarmac Champion once more than his late rival, but Bertie was ahead of Austin in the overall total of Tarmac event victories.

Costs and other commitments have meant that many talented men and women have only touched the sport from time to time, and we could fill another book if we profiled everyone whose name appears on the list of Tarmac winners – people like Brendan Fagan, Demi Fitzgerald, Gabriel Snow and James Leckey, or Tarmac Champions John Coyne (1982) and Ian Greer (1999).

But this book is not meant to be a definitive history of stage rallying in Ireland: it's simply a chance to relive many of the great moments of the sport through Esler Crawford's stunning photographs, and to reminisce about the fun and enjoyment that this remarkable circus has given us over the years. For rally people are party people, and the requirements of social endurance can often be as arduous as the events themselves, as many visitors have discovered.

Will rallying continue to be as popular in the coming years? Will it continue to win the PR battle between its supporters and the people who have to suffer the inconvenience of having their roads closed? Can the balance be maintained between safety requirements and the risks and challenges of the sport? Will the cost of running these monstrous machines finally become too high? It is not possible to predict the answers, but one thing is for sure: in generations to come the names Hopkirk, Curley, Boyd, Coleman, McRae (the honorary Irishman), Meagher, McKinstry, Fisher, McHale and Nesbitt will be remembered as tarmac titans, stars among the many who were 'mad for road'!

ATLANTIC CROSSING

Andrew Nesbitt and co-driver James O'Brien on the Atlantic Drive stage of the 2004 Donegal International Rally. The damage on the rear of their Kenny McKinstry S9 Subaru came about during a controversial incident on the previous stage when rivals Donnelly and McGarrity both hit the stranded Subaru.

Irish Tarmac Champions

Year	Driver	Car
1978	John Taylor	Ford Escort RS1800
1979	Brian Nelson	Ford Escort RS1800
1980	Jimmy McRae	Vauxhall Chevette HSR
1981	Jimmy McRae	Opel Ascona 400
1982	John Coyne	Lotus Sunbeam
1983	Austin McHale	Vauxhall Chevette HSR
1984	Billy Coleman	Opel Manta 400
1985	Austin McHale	Opel Manta 400
1986	Austin McHale	Opel Manta 400
1987	Mark Lovell	Ford Sierra Cosworth
1988	Mark Lovell Terry	Ford Sierra Cosworth
1989	Russell Brookes	Ford Sierra Cosworth
1990	Bertie Fisher	BMW M3
1991	Kenny McKinstry	Ford Sierra Cosworth
1992	Bertie Fisher	Subaru Legacy
1993	Bertie Fisher	Subaru Legacy
1994	Kenny McKinstry	Subaru Legacy
1995	Frank Meagher	Ford Escort Cosworth
1996	Bertie Fisher	Subaru Impreza
1997	Austin McHale	Toyota Celica
1998	Austin McHale	Toyota Celica
1999	Ian Greer	Toyota Celica
2000	Andrew Nesbitt	Subaru Impreza WRC
2001	Not held	(foot-and-mouth disease)
2002	Andrew Nesbitt	Subaru Impreza WRC
2003	Derek McGarrity	Subaru Impreza WRC

First published in 2004 by
Blackstaff Press
4c Heron Wharf, Sydenham Business Park
Belfast BT3 9LE, Northern Ireland

Text © Alan Tyndall
Images © Esler Crawford

Printed in England by The Bath Press

A CIP catalogue record for this book is available from the British Library.

ISBN 0-85640-760-7

www.blackstaffpress.com

The authors wish to thank the following for their help with this book: Andrew Bushe
for invaluable research assistance, Sammy Hamill, Derek Johnston, Robert McBurney,
Bob Montgomery, Paul Phelan, RIAC Archive, Rosemary Smith.

The RIAC, Rosemary Smith and Derek Johnston kindly lent photographs for reproduction.